How to Prepare and Serve a Meal And Interior Decoration

AF621085

by

Lillian B. Lansdown

Double 9 BOOKS

How to Prepare and Serve a Meal And Interior Decoration

by Lillian B. Lansdown

Copyright © 2024

All Rights reserved.

No part of this publication may be reproduced, stored in a retrieval system, or transmitted in any form or by any means, electronic, mechanical, photocopying or Otherwise, without the written permission of the publisher.
The author/editor asserts the moral right to be identified as the author/editor of this work.

ISBN: 978-93-62208-71-2

Published by

DOUBLE 9 BOOKS

2/13-B, Ansari Road
Daryaganj, New Delhi – 110002
info@double9books.com
www.double9books.com
Tel. 011-40042856

This book is under public domain

ABOUT THE AUTHOR

Lillian B. Lansdown is a renowned culinary expert and author whose masterpiece, "How to Prepare and Serve a Meal And Interior Decoration," stands as a comprehensive guide to the art of cooking and home decor. In this seminal work, Lansdown shares her wealth of knowledge and expertise, offering readers practical advice and creative inspiration for creating memorable meals and stylish living spaces. Combining culinary prowess with a keen eye for interior design, Lansdown's book serves as a valuable resource for homemakers and aspiring chefs alike. From mastering basic cooking techniques to arranging elegant table settings and enhancing home interiors, Lansdown's insights empower readers to elevate their culinary and aesthetic skills with confidence and flair. With clear, concise instructions and beautiful illustrations, "How to Prepare and Serve a Meal And Interior Decoration" guides readers through every aspect of meal preparation and home decor, ensuring success in the kitchen and beyond. Lansdown's passion for good food and beautiful living shines through in every page, making this book an indispensable companion for anyone seeking to create memorable dining experiences and stylish living spaces.

CONTENTS

CHAPTER I
BEFORE THE MEAL IS SERVED 7

CHAPTER II
ENTER THE WAITRESS 10

CHAPTER III
BREAKFAST 12

CHAPTER IV
LUNCHEONS 15

CHAPTER V
THE INFORMAL (HOME) DINNER 18

CHAPTER VI
THE FORMAL DINNER 20

CHAPTER VII
AFTERNOON TEAS 24

CHAPTER VIII
SUPPERS 26

CHAPTER IX
OUTSIDE THE EIGHTEENTH AMENDMENT 28

CHAPTER X
CARVING HINTS 30

CHAPTER XI
PLANNING A MENU 31

CHAPTER XII
MENUS FOR A THANKSGIVING—A CHRISTMAS AND A LENTEN DINNER 35

INTERIOR DECORATION

CHAPTER I
LINES AND CURVES ... 38

CHAPTER II
FORM, COLOR AND PROPORTION ... 40

CHAPTER III
INDIVIDUAL ROOMS OF THE HOUSE ... 42

CHAPTER IV
LIVING ROOM, DRAWING ROOM AND LIBRARY ... 44

CHAPTER V
BED ROOM, NURSERY AND PLAY ROOM ... 46

CHAPTER VI
SOME HINTS ANENT PERIOD FURNITURE ... 47

CONCLUSION ... 48

CHAPTER I
BEFORE THE MEAL IS SERVED

Before the meal which is to be served comes from the kitchen by way of the butler's pantry to the dining room, there are many things to be considered. The preparation of the meal (not the process of its cooking, but its *planning* as a composite whole) and all the various details which precede the actual sitting down at the table of those who expect to enjoy it, must be seen to. The preparation of the meal, its *menu*, will be dealt with later, in connection with the meal itself. For the present we will concentrate on its preparatory aspects.

IN THE BUTLER'S PANTRY

The butler's pantry is the connecting link between kitchen and dining room. It is at the same time an arsenal and a reserve line, equipped with requisites to meet all emergencies. The perfect butler's pantry should contain everything, from vegetable brushes for cleaning celery to a galvanized refuse can. In between come matches, bread boards, soap, ammonia and washing soda, a dish drainer, every kind of towel, cheesecloth and holder, strainers (for tea, coffee and punch), ice water, punch and soup pitchers of enamel ware, the tools and seasonings for salad making, cut-glass brushes, and knives of different sizes.

In the butler's pantry the soiled linen should be kept, if possible in a hamper, if not, in a bag. There should also be a towel rack, an electric or hot-water heater for keeping food hot and—we are speaking of the ideal pantry, of course—a small icebox where table butter, cream and salad dressing may be kept, and plates chilled for serving cold dishes. Adding a linen closet with shelves, a chest of drawers (for tablecloths, napkins, doilies, centerpieces, *etc.*) and the necessary shelves for china and glass (hang your cups and save space!), and we may leave the butler's pantry and enter the dining room.

BEFORE ANYTHING EDIBLE COMES TO THE TABLE

We will not waste time on directions regarding the laying of the tablecloth. Only remember that it must form a true line through the center of the table (your "silence cloth" had best be of table padding, a doubled cotton flannel or asbestos) and not hang below the table less than nine inches. The usual arrangement of the centerpiece in the center of the table (the table itself being immediately under the light, unless the waitress is thereby prevented from moving between the table and sideboard) with its dish of fruit or ferns or flowers (never so high as to cut off view or conversation) can be varied to suit individual taste. But the covers (the plates, glasses, napkin and silver of each individual) must always be in line, opposite each other on the opposite sides of the table. The plate doilies indicate the covers when a bare table is laid. The service plate which each person receives stays where put unless it is replaced by a hot plate.

NAPKINS, SILVER, CHINA AND GLASS

Napkins (fold flat and square) lie at the left of the forks. The hem of the napkin, turned up, should parallel the forks and the table edge.

When dinner is served without a maid, everything yields to avoiding leaving the table. In that case put on the dessert silver (which otherwise should not be done) with the other dinner silver. Place all silver in its order of use, and remember that three forks are enough. If more are needed let them appear with the courses which demand them. The quietest and therefore most desirable way of putting the dessert silver on the table, is to serve it from a napkin, from the right. Knives should have their cutting edge toward the plate, at its right, and lie half an inch from the table edge. Spoons, bowls facing upward, lie at the right of the knife; forks at the left of the plate. When shell food is served (clams, oysters or mussels) the fork is placed at the right of the plate. The upper right-hand side of the bread and butter plate is the place for the butter spreader.

In general do not arrange your cover too loosely, and see to it that the glass, china and silver for each cover sets close without the pieces touching. Glasses are placed just above the knives, a little to the right. Neither cups nor glasses should ever be filled to the brim. The bread and butter plate (bread and butter are, as a rule, *not* served with *formal* dinners) somewhat to the left, beyond the service plate. Between each two covers, or just in front of each, place your pepper and salt sets. The salt spoon lies across the open saltcellar.

When the table is set for some impromptu meal at which a knife will not be used, the fork takes the place of the knife at the right-hand side, and the teaspoon is laid beside the fork.

DESIRABLE IMPROVEMENTS

No one wants to see the inner economy of the butler's pantry, nor should the perhaps fragrant but cloying odors of the kitchen be wafted into the dining room whenever the swingdoor of the pantry opens or closes. The screen obviates both disadvantages. Another improvement has been the introduction of the serving table in place of the sideboard. It now conveniently holds all the extras needed for the meal.

CHAPTER II
ENTER THE WAITRESS

The waitress has already been busy, as we have seen, laying the cloth and covers for the meal. Now, however, she must live up more closely to the implied meaning of her name. Either the hostess or the daughter of the family who is acting as waitress, or the waitress herself announces the meal. For informal service, with a member of the family acting as a waitress, the former may quietly leave the table to attend to the bringing on or carrying off of a course, or to supplying water, butter, *etc*. But the same care and attention to everyone's needs is expected of her as of a regular waitress. Water, butter, rolls, bread, *etc*., should never have to be asked for. Within reach of hand the waitress should always have a soft napkin to remove any liquid spilled during the meal, at once covering the spot with a fresh doily. She must see to it that there are hot plates for hot dishes, and chilled plates for cold ones.

THE MAID AT THE TABLE

The waitress should serve and remove everything, except beverages and extra silver from the guest's *left*. Fork and spoon should always be easily at hand for the person served, and dishes should *never* be offered and removed by *reaching across a cover*. Remove glasses, cups and saucers from the *right*, and serve all beverages from the right. Plates should be placed and removed, one by one. Two plates of food (especially salads or soup) may be brought into the dining room at the same time, but *one should be left on the serving table*.

The host is served last, the hostess first, then the guest of honor (at the hostess' right), then the guest at the right of the host, and so on till all have been served.

Waitresses should *not* grasp the edge of the plate or put the thumb over the rim in placing or handling. The left hand should always be used for removing plates. Take away with each course whatever is needed for a later one, large dishes of food, soiled china, glass and silver. Then crumb the table with a small plate and clean, folded napkin.

When serving dishes of food do so with a dinner napkin folded square on the palm of the hand. The serving dish should be held firmly and not too high. If necessary steady with right hand on edge of dish. Close contact with the person served always should be avoided. The serving tray comes into its own for removing or passing cream and sugar, pepper and salt, *etc.* Candies, salted nuts, water and wineglasses stay on the table until the meal is over.

In clearing the table remove glass and silver first, brush up crumbs which may have fallen on the floor, and carefully shake, fold and put away the table linen.

CHAPTER III
BREAKFAST

Breakfast is the first meal of the American day. It should be daintily and deftly served. Fruit, cereal and some main dish (bacon, fish, eggs) together with toast, hot rolls or muffins, coffee, tea or cocoa, are its main essentials. The bare, doilied table is popular for breakfast use.

BREAKFAST FRUIT

Fresh pears, plums, peaches, apricots, nectarines, mandarins and apples are all served in the same manner—on a plate about six inches across, with a silver fruit knife for quartering and peeling. If a waitress serves, fruit knife and plate are placed first, and then the dish containing the fruit is passed.

Berries—raspberries, blackberries, blueberries, strawberries, as also baked apples, stewed fruits (peaches, prunes and apricots) and all cooked fruits, are offered in little fruit dishes on service plates, together with powdered (or fine granulated) sugar and cream. Strawberries are sometimes left unhulled, when of "exhibition" size. They then should be served in apple bowls or plates, with powdered sugar on the side.

In serving grapes, the waitress, after supplying fruit plates, passes a compote containing the grapes and offers fruit shears, so that each guest may cut what he or she desire. Cherries are served in the same manner, with the addition of a finger bowl.

When grapefruit is served, it is usually as a half, the core removed and sugar added, on a fruit plate or in a grapefruit bowl, together with an orange spoon.

Oranges may be served from a compote, whole, and may be eaten cut crosswise in halves, with the orange spoon; or peeled and eaten in sections. If oranges are served peeled and sliced on a fruit plate they may be eaten with a fork. Sugar should always be passed when they are eaten in this way. Orange juice is the extracted juice served in small glasses two-thirds full.

Cantaloupe (filled with cracked ice) and honeydew melon (it is smart to accompany the latter with a slice of lemon) are served in halves or quarters, on fruit plates (or special melon dishes) and eaten with a fruit spoon. Sugar, salt and pepper should be offered with these by the waitress. Watermelon is usually cut in wedges or circles. It should always be served very cold, on a large fruit plate, and with fruit knife and fork. If half-melons are served, with the rind, the host cuts egg-shaped pieces from the fruit, and places it on individual plates for passing by the waitress.

Bananas may be served "in the skin" at breakfast, or peeled and sliced, with sugar and cream, or sprinkled with sugar and lemon juice.

Shredded pineapple, sprinkled with sugar, or sliced pineapple (slices an inch thick) may be served from a large dish by the waitress.

Fruit at breakfast does not *necessarily* demand a waitress. In may be served at each cover before the guests and family seat themselves. It does call for a finger bowl, however. Only when berries or sliced fruits are served can the finger bowl be omitted.

CEREALS

Cereals are a matter of personal taste. Cooked cereals, such as oatmeal, rolled oats, hominy, corn-meal mush and cracked wheat should come on the table hot, and be served in bowls with sugar (brown sugar, if preferred) and cream. Again, the host may serve the cereal from a large porringer, the waitress bringing him the individual bowls, and taking them to the guests when filled. Dry cereals are served in the same way. Puffed grains or flakes gain crispness and flavor when reheated, *not browned*, before serving.

TOAST

The best breakfast toast is that made at the table over an electric toaster. Be sure, if you have French toast, hot cakes or waffles served, that they come from the kitchen *hot*. A perforated silver cover should cover the plate containing them to prevent their cooling. *Never use a soup plate or bowl for the purpose!* The steam cannot escape and the toast grows soggy. Do not forget syrup when waffles, hot cakes or French toast are served. Some prefer cinnamon and sugar to syrup with hot cakes, and they should also be on hand.

BACON

Bacon is the ideal breakfast meat. The rasher of bacon should be served piping hot on a hot silver platter, in crisp, curling slices. Incidentally, it should be just as crisp when it appears with a favorite companion, as "bacon and eggs."

EGGS

Cooked in the shell (medium or soft-boiled) eggs should be served in an egg cup or egg glass, on a plate, and *under cup or glass.* Each egg thus served should be accompanied by a silver egg cutter and (unless there is plenty of silver at the cover) a silver spoon.

A vegetable dish or a small plate will do for the hard-boiled egg.

Poached eggs appear in individual shirred egg dishes, to the left of each cover, on small plates with service spoon.

Scrambled eggs are served in individual portions, as above; or distributed by the host from a large platter, and passed by the waitress.

Omelet should be served on a large platter with hot individual service plates before the host. The waitress may pass the individual portions or—it is customary with scrambled eggs—they may be passed from host to guest around the table.

COFFEE

Coffee is the favorite and logical breakfast drink, though some prefer tea, cocoa and milk. The breakfast coffee service should be placed before the hostess. In its most attractive form it comprises a large silver tray, which holds coffee (or percolator), the hot-water pot, creamer, sugar bowl with tongs, and cups and saucers. (There may also be a bowl for the water used to heat the cups.) When tea is the breakfast beverage the samovar takes the place of the percolator.

The large silver service platter may be dispensed with, if desired, in favor of a tile to hold the coffee urn, the other components of the service being grouped about it. There is a charming touch of intimacy about coffee made at the table with an electric percolator, poured by the hostess and passed at the table (or by a waitress). When the hostess pours she should at the same time ask the guest's preferences (those of members of the family are supposed to be known) as regards cream and sugar. Cream and sugar always enter the cup *first*! The true coffee-drinker at once notices a difference in flavor if the coffee first be poured, and the cream and sugar added.

FOR THE CHILDREN

If the children eat breakfast with the family, a regular child's service, with attractive little knives and spoons should be provided, and his whole service, preferably, should be arranged on a tray near the table's edge. Every child likes to have his own porridge bowl, his mug and little milk pitcher, and having his own table tools teaches him to be neat and self-reliant.

CHAPTER IV
LUNCHEONS

THE INFORMAL LUNCHEON

The informal luncheon or lunch—originally the light meal eaten between breakfast and dinner, but now often taking the place of dinner, the fashionable hour being one (or half after if cards are to follow)—is of two kinds. The "buffet" luncheon, at which the guests eat standing; and the luncheon served at small tables, at which the guests are seated. (In general all that is here said with regard to the "buffet" luncheon, applies to the "buffet" supper or evening "spread." The only actual difference is that lighted candles may be used at an evening luncheon, and that the daytime luncheon may offer courses more variegated and solid in character than would be suitable for evening eating.)

Plates, silver and napkins are conveniently arranged on a laid table in the case of the "buffet" lunch. One or two hot and one or two cold dishes (according to the number of guests who are to be fed), and one or two iced desserts with one cream or jelly in mold should be sufficient. The knife is tabooed at the "buffet" lunch, hence all the food must be such as can be eaten with fork or spoon. As a rule, friends of the hostess serve (host and hostess may help), though, if convenient, waitresses may see to the wants of the guests. To keep the table from looking crowded, maids may replenish the dishes from pantry or serving table as may be necessary. Plates of sandwiches or filled rolls (not too far from the table edge) olives and relishes should also be arranged on the table, though cakes, candies and salted nuts may be passed by the maids. The rolls go with the hot course, the sandwiches with the salad. When a "buffet" lunch is served at a big reception, with any number of guests coming and going, all the buffet refreshments should appear on the table at the same time.

The following dishes cover the essentials of a "buffet" luncheon. Beverages: punch, coffee, chocolate (poured from urn, or filled cups brought from pantry on tray); hot entrées of various sorts (served from chafing dish or platter) preceded by hot bouillon; cold entrées, salads, lobster, potatoes, chicken, shrimp, with heavy dressings; hot rolls, wafer-cut sandwiches (lettuce, tomato, deviled ham, *etc.*); small cakes, frozen creams and ices.

The informal luncheon at small tables calls for service by a number of maids, hence the "buffet" plan is preferable.

THE FORMAL LUNCHEON

A "luncheon set" (a luncheon cloth or center-piece with doilies of the same color and design) or a bare table may be used for the formal luncheon, with special luncheon napkins, in a three-cornered fold. Butter is not usually served, the individual dishes (filled) are placed at the top of the plate without doily, and if a "cup" of some sort is to be served, an apollinaris glass is placed a little below the water glass. Bread and rolls had best be passed, though they may be placed in or on a napkin, instead of a bread dish. Favors, if used, should appear at the top of the plate, or grouped about the center-piece, with connecting ribbons to the plates. This is an attractive form of arrangement. Dishes of candies and bonbons (with bonbon spoon beside them) are placed on the table at will, wherever they make the best appearance, but large dishes with spoon must be taken from the serving table and passed.

THE FORMAL LUNCHEON MENU

The cocktail is the preliminary entering wedge of the formal luncheon. Some hostesses serve a light cocktail with very thin sandwiches or wafers in their drawing room before luncheon proper is served. At the latter the fruit cocktail (served on small plate, with doily, glass and spoon) or a Lobster or Scallop Cocktail (oyster fork) is followed by the first course.

Here there is a wide choice—Cream of Pea soup with or without croutons, Lobster Bisque, Mock Turtle, Consommé (Parmesan or Chicken), White Soup with Wine—whatever best fits in with the general scheme of the luncheon may be served. The handles of the bouillon cup, when it is placed before the guest, should parallel the edge of the table.

The passing of Bread Sticks, Olives and Radishes should precede the removal of the bouillon cup, and the placing before the guest of the warmed plates for the fish. Here we have the same embarrassment of riches. Deviled Crabs, Fried Sardines, Fish Cutlets with Dutch Sauce, Fried Shad Roe, Oyster and Mushroom Patties, Halibut in any style, together with rolls (passed in napkins) and Dressed Cucumbers will answer for the fish course.

Before the meat course the claret cup should be poured, the waitress ready with napkin in her left hand to catch any drops which may spill from the pitcher. We will merely indicate five choices for the *pièce de résistance* of the formal luncheon. 1. Fillets of Beef, with Raisin Sauce, Parisian Potatoes (ball-shaped) and French Peas. 2. Broiled Wild Duck, Curried Vegetables, and Currant Jelly Sauce. 3. Fried Chicken with Tomato Mayonnaise, Steamed New Potatoes and Boiled Green Corn. 4. Squab Breasts larded around hot ripe Olives, with Brown Sauce, and Potato Croquettes with Peas. 5. Roast Saddle of Venison, with Sauté Potato Balls and Broiled Tomatoes with Horseradish Hollandaise Sauce. None of these combinations should disappoint a formal luncheon guest. When this course is over, the salad should be substituted for the dinner plate which has been removed.

The salad is by no means the least attractive among the courses. You may have Pepper and Fruit Salad, with Nut-Bread Sandwiches or an Asparagus Salad with Lemon Rings. You may incline to Spring Salad with Horseradish Sandwiches or to Dressed Lettuce with Cheese-Bread Wafers. Or, again, you may prefer Chicory Salad with Cheese Croquettes. You have but to choose. With the passing of the salad and its sandwiches, salt and pepper sets are removed, the table is crumbed and the ice-cream plates are laid out, together with ice-cream forks and spoons.

Will you have Maroon Ice Cream with Sponge Drops or a Tutti-Frutti Ice? Canton Mousse with Cream Cones, or Orange Cream Sherbet with Chocolate Petits Fours? Chocolate Parfait with Lady Fingers or Frozen Neapolitan Charlotte with Marshmallow Wafers? You must exercise your individual choice among these and a hundred others.

The passing of the finger-bowl service (plate, bowl and doily) precedes the appearance of the demi-tasse, and the passing of candies and bonbons. (At less formal luncheons, the hostess pours the coffee at the table. When this is done the service usually is placed before her when the dessert course ends.)

The more formal luncheon dictates that coffee be served in the drawing room. Here the waitress passes the after-dinner coffee which the hostess pours. If it seems preferrable to serve coffee at the table, the waitress, after she has placed the finger-bowl service, puts the coffee at the guest's left hand, and passes him cream and sugar. When he has removed his finger bowl the guest uses the plate for his bonbons.

CHAPTER V
THE INFORMAL (HOME) DINNER

The setting of the table for the home dinner follows the general rules already given. As it is a quite informal affair, however, the side dish (never seen at a formal dinner) is permissible. Dessert, too, may be served in a small dish set in a plate. A carving cloth (for *paterfamilias* usually carves at the home dinner) protects the tablecloth from spatters and bits of crisp fat which the most skillful carver cannot always avoid sending over the dish.

If a maid serves, she should always have an extra plate, one more than the number of individuals to be served. She will need it.

A salad served with meat, at an informal dinner, is placed on the right side, *from the right*, the exception to the rule of serving from the left.

Vegetables, once served, are taken back to the kitchen, to keep them warm. If a second serving is desired, the mistress rings. Suit yourself about having the serving silver placed on the table *before* the dish to be served is carried in. The latest wrinkle—and it is a time and step-saving one—dictates that the silver be brought in on a platter. The soup, to be served hot (it should always be served in soup plates at dinner and never in bouillon cups) must be brought in after the family have taken their places.

A family dinner may be served quite comfortably even without a maid. The table set and the service laid, the younger members of the family should attend to her duties. One may bring in the soup, hot, in individually heated plates. Another may fill the water glasses, pass butter or sauces and remove dishes between courses. The most convenient way of serving vegetables, under these circumstances, is for some member of the family next the carver to attend to it, as soon as meat has been laid on the plate. It saves extra passing. See to it that too many things—butter, salt, pepper, cream, sauces, *etc.*—are not traveling about the table at once. All the formal features of the more formal meals may be dropped or modified to suit individual needs or circumstances in the informal home dinner.

TWELVE MENUS FOR GOOD FAMILY DINNERS

1. Corn Mock Bisque. Roast Chicken with Bread Stuffing, Giblet Gravy. Boiled Rice. Sauté Egg Plant. Stuffed Green Peppers. Prune Pudding. Black Coffee.

2. Onion Soup. Fried Smelts, Sauce Tartare. Broiled Porterhouse Beefsteak. Maître d'Hotel Butter (1/4 cup butter, 1/2 teaspoonful salt, 1/8 teaspoonful pepper, tablespoonful lemon juice, 1 ditto parsley, fine chopped; work butter in bowl with wooden spoon till creamy, then add other ingredients slowly). Potato Strips. Creamed Turnips. Steamed Chocolate Pudding, Sterling Sauce.

3. Carrot Soup. Braised Beef. Boiled Potatoes with Butter and Parsley. Fried Parsnips. Onion Soufflé. Spiced Apples à la Lyman (6 large apples, 3/4 cup sugar, 1 teaspoonful cinnamon, 1/4 teaspoonful salt, 1/4 cup water: arrange cored and pared apples in baking dish, mix sugar, salt and cinnamon and fill cavities. Add water, bake till apples are soft, basting repeatedly with syrup in dish. Remove, cool, pile meringue on top of each apple. Back to oven and bake for eight minutes. Chill and serve with sugar and cream). Black coffee.

4. Huntington Soup and Celery. Braised Leg of Mutton. Mashed Sweet Potatoes. Beets, Sauce Piquant. Stuffed Tomato Salad, Boiled Dressing. Cream Jelly.

5. Onion Soup. Beefsteak à la Henrietta Sauté Potato Balls, Mashed Turnips. Cheese Salad. Coffee Sponge.

6. Corn and Chicken Soup. Braised Fowl, Chestnut Stuffing. Duchess Potatoes, Fried Tomatoes (Parmesan). Honeycomb Pudding, Creamy Sauce. Coffee.

7. Brown Soup with Macaroni Rings. Creamed Mushrooms. Roast Leg of Veal. Mashed Potatoes. Brussels Sprouts with Celery. Asparagus Salad. Fruit Tapioca. Coffee.

8. Clam Bouillon. Boiled Leg of Mutton, Caper Sauce, Mashed Potatoes, Fried Cucumbers. Peach Cabinet Pudding. Crackers and Cheese. Black Coffee.

9. Broiled Fish, Cold Slaw in Cabbage Shell. Stuffed Hearts with Vegetables. Potatoes Goldenrod, Almond Pudding, Whipped Cream. Assorted Fruit. Coffee.

These are samples of what is possible in the way of tasty combinations for the informal family dinner.

CHAPTER VI
THE FORMAL DINNER

From the informal dinner in which the family waits on itself, to the formal dinner, at which two waitresses attend to the comfort of the diners, is but a step. Yet it is a serious one for the hostess who gives the latter form of dinner. The cook often requires extra help (dishwashing, *etc.*); and where a chambermaid is available, she has to be drafted as a second waitress or an extra waitress engaged. There must be a helper on duty in the pantry, for there must be no hitch in any detail of the formal dinner service. So the extra pantry-hand must serve soup and pour coffee, see that there is crushed ice always ready, stack up soiled dishes, open wine bottles (yes, this is still done!) and be prepared to do anything else which will help make the dinner a success.

THE WHAT'S WHAT OF A FORMAL DINNER

The fine damask tablecloth is a feature—though the table is set practically as though for a formal luncheon—and large-size dinner napkins are the rule. The parsnips of circumstance are not buttered at the formal dinner, though the bread and butter plate sometimes shows its face as a serving convenience for bread, celery, olives and radishes. Wineglasses still appear in formal dinners given *in private*. This provides for quite an array of glassware. At the point of the knives, in the following order stand the water goblet and the iced tea glass or appolinaris glass. The wineglasses (usually no more than three wines are served) are grouped to the right of the water goblet. Their order is that of use. (There are separate glasses for high and low cocktail, sherry, sauterne, claret, champagne, cordials and whiskey.) Each guest has his own nut dish, placed directly before him. Candles are lit and water glasses half-filled a few minutes in advance of the dinner announcement, and the hostess already having arranged place cards before this is done.

THE COURSES

The "initial" course may be placed on the table before dinner is announced or may be served after. If, however, you serve cocktails in the drawing room with the accompanying caviar or lettuce sandwiches, or if you serve a canapé, do not repeat the latter as the opening of the dinner. For instance, you should not serve a Lobster Canapé in the drawing room and a Finnan Haddie Canapé at the dinner table. Fruit cocktails of every kind, and canapés are in order for this commencement of the meal.

A GOOD FRUIT COCKTAIL RECIPE

Mix shredded pineapple, halved strawberries, (fresh, not preserved), with grapefruit pulp, the pulp in a two to one proportion to the pineapple, chill and cover with wine dressing. To be served in champagne glass, with top garnish of a large strawberry for each glass.

The soup course may be preceded by one of fruit, where the cocktail or canapé has been served in the drawing room. Supposing it to be strawberries, the berries will already be waiting in a small plate when the guests take their seats upon entering the dining room. They should be unhulled, large, selected berries, and may be eaten either by hand (dipped in the sugar mound into which they are thrust on the plate) or with the strawberry fork. The serving of a finger bowl with this course is a matter of taste.

When this course has been removed, the soup is served, and the head waitress pours the sherry, while cakes and olives are passed by a second waitress.

If fish comes next—we will presume the fish to be Shad à la Delmonico, Halibut à la Meniere or Turbans of Flounder—it is passed in the platter, followed by rolls and Cucumber Ribbons, Dressed Cucumbers or Sliced Cucumbers, as the case may be. Then the fish course is taken from the table and we come to the entrée.

If one entrée is the limit it precedes the roast. Where you have two entrées the heavy (meat) entrée comes first, then the lighter (vegetable) one. Let us say we have only Delmonico Tomatoes or Mushroom Croquettes. We would carry on next with our roast fowl or flesh. But if we have Oyster and Mushroom Patties *and* Roast Ham with Cider Sauce as entrées, the Roast Ham, being the heavier, should be served first.

Our roast—the champagne was poured from the *right* side with the *right* hand *after* the removal of the fish plates—is now due. The entrée plates in turn have been taken away and the warm dinner plates substituted for them. Ah, the roast! What shall it be? There is so much from which to choose. It cannot be too epicurean for a formal dinner. Fillet of Beef Larded with Truffles, with a Brown Mushroom Sauce; Crown of Lamb (crowned with Green Peas and surrounded by Fried Potato Balls); Roast Turkey with Truffle Gravy; Venison Saddle, Chateaubriand of Beef, Sirloin Steak, there is no lack of choice.

When both roast and game are served, a frozen punch is supposed to draw the line of demarcation between them, and the salad enters *with* the game instead of being counted as an individual course.

While one waitress passes the roast, another follows with the potatoes. Other vegetables and rolls then come in order and, if the nut dishes of any of the guests are empty, they are refilled.

When more than a single meat course is served at a formal dinner, the sorbets and frozen punches should be dropped. In such a case they are only permissible at an especially large official dinner, a banquet or a large hotel spread.

After dinner plates have been taken away the salad (already arranged on the plate, the fork on the right hand side) is served from the right, and sandwiches are passed. The variety of possible salads has already been alluded to in the consideration of the formal luncheon, hence nothing need be added here on that head.

With the emptied salad plate are removed peppers and salts (on tray) and the table crumbed, the ice cream plate (as at the formal luncheon) is placed. The ice cream mold is passed with *the mold already cut, but retaining its shape,* to facilitate the guest's helping himself. Together with the ice cream, the accompanying small cakes are passed.

The appearance of the finger bowl service follows the removal of the dessert plates. The finger bowl should be approximately one-fourth full of luke-warm water (never cold) and garnished. The dessert plate is removed with the left hand, the plate, finger bowl, and doily served with the left. The passing of the bonbons concludes the actual service at the table.

Coffee, as already mentioned, is poured by the hostess in the drawing room and, after the waitress has collected and removed the coffee service (and cups and saucers) she may, in the event that cordials are served, return with the cordial service, which the hostess pours and the waitress serves as in the case of the coffee.

If the ladies *only* retire to the drawing room, one waitress serves them there with coffee, while another remains in the dining room. Here she passes cigars and cigarettes on a tray, together with a lighted candle or matches, and then serves coffee and cordials or brandy and soda.

It is good form for the waitress to serve carbonated water in apollinaris glasses in the drawing room about an hour after the conclusion of the dinner.

THREE FORMAL DINNER MENUS

1. Grapefruit. Chicken Consommé with Oysters. Bread Sticks (served like roll in napkin). Deviled Crabs. Chicken Mousse with Sauterne Jelly. Saddle of Mutton. White Potato Croquettes. Carrots and Turnips a la Poulette. Currant Mint Sorbet. Mushrooms au Casserole. Roast Grouse, Bread Sauce. Watercress Salad. Willard Soufflé. Strawberry Ice Cream. Salted Almonds. Bonbons. Crackers and Cheese. Black Coffee.

2. Oyster Cocktail. Saltines. Mushroom and Sage Soup. Dinner Braids. Lobster Chops. Cucumber Boats. Sauce Tartare. Swedish Timbales with Calf's Brains. Larded Fillet of Beef with Truffles. Brown Mushroom Sauce, Potato Rings. Flageolets. Buttered Carrots. Asparagus Jelly with Pistachio Bisque. Ice Cream. Cream Sponge Balls. Salted Almonds. Bonbons. Water Thins. Neufchâtel Cheese. Black Coffee. (From "A Book of Good Dinners for My Friend": Fannie Merrit Farmer.)

3. Cocktails. Caviar Sandwiches. Selected Strawberries. Mock Bouillon. Olives. Sherry. Rolled Cassava Cakes. Turbans of Flounder. Dressed Cucumbers. Rolls. Delmonico Tomatoes. Roasted Incubator Chickens. Chantilly Asparagus Potatoes. Buttered Asparagus Tips. Champagne. Grapefruit and Alligator Pear Salad, Paprika Crackers. Montrose Pudding. Small Cakes. Coffee. Cordials. (From "Table Service," Lucy G. Allen).

CHAPTER VII
AFTERNOON TEAS

Afternoon teas are of two kinds, formal and informal, and the informal outdoor tea in the open, on the lawn or in the garden, is a variant of the latter variety. Here the tea wagon comes into play, and tea is often tea in name only, since at summer outdoor teas not only iced tea, but iced coffee, iced chocolate or punch are often served.

THE INFORMAL TEA

Do not set a table for the informal tea. The tea service is merely brought to the sun parlor, drawing room or living room in which the tea is to be served, and placed on the table. There the hostess makes and pours the tea, unless she prefers to have it brought in on a tea tray already made for pouring.

The tea service comprises: a teakettle for boiling water with filled alcohol lamp and matches; a tea caddy with teaspoon and (if only a few cups are to be made) a tea ball. A tea creamer, cut sugar, a saucer of sliced lemon, and cups and saucers with spoon on cup saucer, as well as tea napkins complete the service. The water brought in in the teakettle should be hot. If this precaution is observed, the tea will boil very soon after the lamp is lighted. The sandwiches served at an informal afternoon tea should be very simple: lettuce, olive or nut butter, or plain bread and butter, nor should the small cakes also passed be elaborate or rich.

THE FORMAL TEA

The formal tea—a tea becomes formal as soon as cards are sent out for it—is a very different affair. As many as four ladies may pour, two during the first, and two during the second hour. Friends of the hostess—they serve all refreshments, though waitresses assist, removing soiled cups and plates and bringing in fresh ones—preside at either table end, and the table is decorated (flowers and candles). At one end of the luncheon cloth (or the table may be laid with doilies) stands the service tray, with teapot, hot-water pot, creamer, sugar bowl with tongs and cut sugar, and sliced lemons in dish with lemon fork. The tray also contains cup and saucers (each saucer with spoon, handle paralleling cup). The coffee, bouillon or chocolate service is established in the same manner at the other end of the table. If coffee is served, the service tray is equipped with urn, cream and sugar; if chocolate, whipped cream in bowl with ladle; if bouillon, the urn alone.

Each lady who pours must have a large napkin convenient to guard her gown. Arranged along the table should be plates of sandwiches and cakes, bonbon dishes and dishes with salted nuts. But the table must not be crowded. This important rule is responsible for the existence of the frappé table.

The frappé table holds the afternoon tea punch. Since the dining room is apt to be well filled as it is, the frappé table had best be established in some other room. On its luncheon cloth is set the punch or frappé bowl with ladle, and individual ices, frozen creams (not too rich or elaborate) or punch are served in frappé or punch bowls by a friend of the hostess. The small plates on which the frappé glasses are served should be piled on the table with doilies (*linen always*) between the plates. When served, the glass is filled with the sherbet or cream, and a sherbet spoon laid at the right-hand side of plate (a tray of sherbet spoons belongs to the frappé table equipment, as well as a filled cake basket, dishes of candy, piles of small plates and small linen napkins). Unless you are entertaining guests to the number of a hundred or more, *never use paper doilies at a formal afternoon tea*!

A pretty custom dictates that young girl friends of the hostess serve the guests. They provide the latter with plate and napkin, ask their choice of beverage, and serve it, together with sandwiches and cakes. Or the plates and napkins may be handed the guests as they enter by a waitress stationed at the door, before they are served by the young girls.

A salad should never be offered at a formal afternoon tea! To do so is to commit a social solecism.

CHAPTER VIII
SUPPERS

Supper, "the evening meal," the last of the day, in modern usage often is actually a dinner, the most elaborate meal; the place of the former dinner being taken by the luncheon. A supper is often a particularly elaborate dinner or banquet, as, for instance, the "class supper."

THE LATE SUPPER

The late supper, often given after a theatre party, or a card party, is always an informal affair. Its favorite form is what might be called the "chafing dish supper," where should they wish, the guests may help themselves.

Two chafing dishes or one may grace the table (laid with luncheon cloth or luncheon set, flowers and candles) according to the number of guests. The chafing dish is set before the hostess on a metal tray resting on an asbestos mat. A teakettle of boiling water, an electric toaster (the asbestos mat of the chafing dish laid over the flame may also be used for keeping toast or croutons made in the kitchen warm while on the table), and plates already heated go with the chafing dish. Also, near at hand, should be matches, an extra napkin, a "sampling" fork and spoon, and a bowl of some sort for burned matches and the "sampling silver."

All that is to be cooked, dry or liquid, should already have been measured and be ready for use. All bowls, small dishes and pitchers containing ingredients for any one dish should be grouped on a single tray, at the left of the person attending to the chafing dish.

Chafing-dish rarebits may be of every kind, and every rarebit should have some main dominating flavor, as green or red pepper, onion, tomato, *etc.* Cheese souffles or sweet souffles are also successful chafing-dish products, as well as cooked fish heated in a piquant sauce.

For chafing-dish purposes there are available: *Meats*: Beef, Venison, Lamb, Cooked Tongue, Bacon and Ham, Chicken, Chicken Livers and Sweetbreads. *Sea Food*: Lobster, Terrapin, Crab Meat, Frogs' Legs, Oysters,

Shrimps, Scallops, Sardines, Salmon and Finnan Haddie. Eggs, Cheese, Tomatoes, Mushrooms and Peas should also be included with this list.

Sliced and toasted bread or crackers heated usually form the basis of the chafing-dish preparation. Rarebits suppose toast or crackers, but creamed dishes demand toast. The chafing dish also pays homage to the sweet tooth in the shape of fudges (Ginger, Nut Raisin, Peanut Butter, Marshmallow, *etc.*); and hot coffee, wine cup, mineral water, beer, ale and cider are the customary chafing-dish supper drinkables.

CHAPTER IX
OUTSIDE THE EIGHTEENTH AMENDMENT

From the alcoholic beverages of the chafing-dish supper to those of the dinner is a natural transition. At the formal dinner wines often accompany the courses and, as already mentioned, liqueurs and cordials supply the final liquid note after the coffee. The theory of alcoholic beverages at the formal dinner is a simple one. Certain fixed and definite rules obtain and are generally observed. Three wines may be served, though the best social form prefers one or two.

SHERRY OR MADEIRA

Sherry or Madeira may accompany the soup course. They should be poured *after* the soup has been placed, and served from a decanter. In general wine should always be poured slowly, and glasses should be filled only two-thirds. The etiquette is for the waitress to pour a little wine into the host's glass, then filling the glasses beginning at the host's right. Sherry should always be served cold, at a temperature of 40° Fahrenheit; the Madeira may be served at a temperature of 65° F., or that of the room.

SAUTERNE OR RHINE WINE

Sauterne or Rhine Wine go with the fish course. They are poured, like the Claret, at the end of the preceding course, before the next course comes on. They (like Sparkling Burgundy and Champagne) are served from the bottle, and the bottle should be held in a folded napkin or bottle holder. The mean average temperature of Sauterne should be 50° F. Some prefer it decidedly cold (chilled in the icebox), others only slightly cold. Rhine Wine should always be cold: 40° F.

CLARET

Claret is the wine for the entrée and, as a rule, is served from a claret pitcher. Being a light wine, it may be served *with* the Champagne and *instead* of it to those who do not prefer the Mumm. Claret should be poured at the end of the course *immediately* before the one with which it is served. The room temperature or one of 65° F. is the proper one for Claret.

CHAMPAGNE, BURGUNDY OR PORT

These wines are served with the meat courses. In order that Champagne or Sparkling Burgundy may come on the table at the proper temperature (Champagne 35° and Burgundy 70° F.) it must be ice-packed for several hours before serving. Care must be taken, however, that it does not frappé when, if required at short notice, it is salt-and-ice packed half an hour before serving. Sweet Champagne, on the other hand, is improved in flavor if slightly frappéed. It should always be served very cold. Like Sauterne, Champagne and Burgundy are served from the bottle. In serving them the wire should be cut, and the cork carefully *worked* out of the bottle by pressing it up with the thumbs. It is wise to work out the cork *under the edge of the table,* since it is sometimes projected with much power. The temperature for Port is 55° F.

CORDIALS AND LIQUEURS

Cordial glasses holding a small quantity are used for serving these sweet, aromatic beverages. Cordials are served plain, with crushed ice or with cream. In serving Crême de Menthe the straw is unusual in private home service, though customary in some hotels. Crême de Menthe glasses should be filled two-thirds full with fine crushed ice, then a little of the cordial poured over it. Chartreuse (green or yellow), Benedictine, Grenadine, Apricot Brandy, Curacoa, and Dantzig Eau de Vie arc usually served without additions or ice. Benedictine or Crême de Cacoa, however, may be served with a dash of plain or whipped cream. The exceedingly sweet Crême Yvette should be served with cracked ice, like Crême de Menthe. Noyau, Kirschwasser, Maraschino and Grenadine may be served as cordials, or reserved for the flavoring of puddings, ices and sauces.

CHAPTER X
CARVING HINTS

Whether it be the waitress or the master of the house who carves, a firm hand, an appraising eye and a sharp carving knife are needed. Some of the chief carving points for roasts are worth knowing.

Beefsteak (Porterhouse): Carve in two pieces, cutting tenderloin and sirloin from the middle bone. Cut in uniformly thick slices, serving a piece for a portion, rare, medium or well done, as may be preferred. *Rib or Sirloin Roast*: Hold firmly, skin side up. Carve in thin, parallel slices, from crisp edge to bone, then slip knife under slices and cut from bones. *Rump Steak*: Cut in thin, parallel slices with grain of meat. Serve like rib or sirloin with dish gravy for each portion. *Fillet of Beefs*: Cut across diagonally, beginning at thick end. Slices should be no more than half an inch thick. *Leg of Lamb*: With rounding side up, plunge carving fork in center of roast, and cut in thin, parallel slices *across grain* to bone. Boned leg of lamb is more easily carved. *Saddle of Mutton*: Make cuts parallel to backbone, half to three-quarters inch apart; then crosscuts at right angles to former, two to two and a half inches long. Slip knife beneath bone to free meat. *Loin of Veal or Lamb*: Cut backbone of each rib before cooking. Cut roast between ribs, serving one for a portion. Carve *Crown of Lamb* in the same way. *Roast Turkey or Roast Chicken, Capon or Guinea Hen*: With bird on back, insert carving fork across highest point of breastbone. Holding it here firmly, cut through skin between second joint and body, close to the latter. Pull back leg and second joint in one piece with knife; disjoint, then cut off wing. Breast meat must be carved in thin, parallel slices. Use knife to part second joints from drumsticks and carve them in slices. Always complete carving one side of a bird before carving the other. Light meat and dark meat, together with stuffing, should be included in each portion, unless a preference is indicated. *Broilers*: Should be cut in halves, and the halves halved, severing at joints. According to size of broiler a quarter or a half is served as an individual portion. *Domestic Duck*: Bird on back (drumsticks to right of carver, as with all fowl) the carving fork is thrust through breast. The joints lie much farther back than those of chickens or turkeys. After removing leg and wing, make cuts in breast meat parallel to breastbone, three-quarters of an inch apart, and remove by sliding knife under meat. Small pieces of rich meat, dark, may be cut from the sides of the duck. *Game Duck*: First cut breast meat from one side, then from other. Half a breast is the individual portion. Legs and wings are too tough, as a rule, for satisfactory table use.

CHAPTER XI
PLANNING A MENU

Food value and contrast—the avoidance of duplicating flavors—are main points in menu planning. An elaborate menu must alternate its light and heavy courses.

SOUP

Thin soups for formal dinners, cream or thick soups for informal ones is the rule. With Consommé, Bread or Cheese Sticks; with thick soups Crackers or Croutons; with Oyster Stew, Oyster Crackers are the proper thing. Soup garnishings (clear soup) include: Shredded Sprouts, Boiled Macaroni cut in rings, Noodles, Lemon Slices, Italian Pastes and Grated Parmesan Cheese, and Sliced Cooked Chestnuts and Royal Custard. Radishes, Celery and Olives are served *after* the soup.

HORS D'OEVRES

Cocktails or Canapés beginning a dinner call for plain sandwiches or wafers. When Oysters or Clams (or any seafood cocktails) are served, Graham or Brown Bread Sandwiches are grateful. With oysters served raw on shell, a Horseradish Sandwich is proper. Tabasco, Grated Horseradish, Catsup, Cayenne, or Cocktail Sauce are in order for oysters or clams, and a half lemon should *always* be laid on the oyster plate.

FISH

Fish flavoring's include Lemon Juice (lemon sliced with or without the rind, or served in quarters or halves) or Tarragon Vinegar. Sauce Tartare is always appropriate for fried fish. Broiled Halibut or Pompano gain by a Sauce Hollandaise. With Baked or Broiled Shad Cucumber Cream Sauce is in order. Broiled fish in general should be mated with rich, heavy sauces, and may be accompanied by Boiled Potato Balls, and Maître d'Hotel butter. When Halibut or Flounder are steamed or baked in fillets, they call for a piquantly flavored sauce: Caper, Brown Tomato, Shrimp or Lobster. Drawn Butter Sauce, Caper or Hollandaise Sauce, are best with Boiled Hot Salmon;

Green Mayonnaise, Vinaigrette or Sauce Tartare with Cold Boiled Salmon. Vegetables do not properly accompany fish in a dinner of many courses. Yet broiled fish may be served with Corn and Shell Beans; white fish of various sorts with Tomatoes, stuffed or fried; and Salmon with Peas.

ENTREES

Every entrée should have the sauce which properly befits it. Patties, however, are not served with the rolls which accompany other entrées, their pastry taking its place. A Purée of Peas may be offered with meat croquettes.

SALADS

For simply dressed salads Cheese Balls or croquettes are appropriate. Fruit salads require thin, unsugared crackers—they may be served hot, sprinkled with mild paprika over butter. Anything of the sort served with a salad is merely served to *bring out* its flavor, not to destroy it!

DESSERTS

When the dinner is a heavy or elaborate one the heavy pudding with a rich sauce is distinctly out of keeping. Frappéed or cold desserts are the proper thing, served together with small wafers or cakes. At less formal dinners the sweet dessert may be omitted, and cheese and hard crackers, a fruit salad, or toasted wafers and coffee may be substituted.

THE ROASTS

Under this head we will list for the reader's convenience a grouping of roasts, together with the sauces and vegetables with which they may be combined for menu purposes in a natural and satisfactory manner.

Beefsteak and Roast Beef: As sauces, Mushroom Sauce is appropriate for both; then for Beefsteak we have Sauce Bearnaise, and Maître d'Hotel Butter; for the Roast Beef, Horseradish Sauce, Banana Sauce and as an accompanying dish, Yorkshire Pudding. Accompanying vegetables for both include: Potatoes, white and sweet, Lima and String Beans, Macaroni, Corn, Peas, Spinach and Onions, Eggplant and Squash, Brussels Sprouts, Cauliflower and Tomatoes.

Boiled Beef: Horseradish Sauce is the preferred one, and Dumplings may accompany it. Potatoes (white), Parsnips, Turnips, Carrots are the first concomitants.

Corned Beef: Plain Boiled Potatoes and Cabbage are the first concomitants. Spinach or Dandelion Greens, Parsnips, Beets, Turnips and Carrots are also indicated.

Roast Lamb: May be accompanied by Banana Croquettes or Bananas baked, by Currant Jelly, Mint Sauce, Mint Jelly or Mint Sherbet. In addition to most of the vegetables already listed, Asparagus, and Jerusalem Artichokes are in order, and Cauliflower may be served with Cream Sauce or *au gratin*.

Lamb Chops Broiled: Potatoes in any form desired, Cauliflower or Brussels Sprouts, and practically any green vegetables, *but piquantly served*, are in order.

Boiled Lamb and Mutton: Caper Sauce and accompanying Dumplings are in order for both. Potatoes (white) Carrots, Turnips and Parsnips are the vegetables.

Saddle of Mutton: Takes all vegetables served with Lamb. It should be served with Currant Jelly or Mint Sauce and, aside from Asparagus, Spinach, French Peas and String Beans, may be accompanied by Fried Rice Balls or Rice Croquettes.

Fowl in General and Chicken: These take Cranberry Jelly and Sauce, also Chestnut, Mushroom, Oysters, Celery and Curry Sauce, and fresh Celery. Glazed Sweet Potatoes, Corn Fritters, Croquettes (Rice, Chestnut, Hominy), all fresh summer vegetables, including String and Lima Beans, Mushrooms, Onions and Squash are in order with fowl.

Roast Turkey: Here, while we may have Cranberry Sauce or Jelly, we *must* have crisp, fresh Celery. There is a choice of stuffings —Sausage, Chestnut, Oyster, Sage and Nut. Potatoes (white and sweet), Brussels Sprouts and Cauliflower, Squash, Turnips and Onions are the vegetables.

Roast Goose: The vegetables are the same as for Roast Turkey, and Brown Giblet Gravy, Apple Sauce and Celery are accompaniments. The stuffings mentioned for Turkey are also in order here.

Duck (Domestic): The vegetables served for all fowl, plus Fried Hominy if desired, are indicated. Either Boiled or Souffléd Onions are a tradition with duck.

Duck (Game): Salads are preferred to vegetables as an accompaniment for Wild Duck. The Salad Greens—any salad green may be used—should be dressed in a simple manner. If preferred, Olive and Orange Jellies and Sauces, and Currant and Plum Jellies, Orange and Cress or Orange and Walnut on Lettuce may be served.

Roast Grouse or Guinea Hen: With Bread Sauce may be served Potatoes (as croquettes or French fried), Celery Croquettes, String Beans, Asparagus, and French Peas, also Currant Jelly and Currant Jelly Sauce.

Quail, Roasted or Broiled: Green salads in which Orange dominates should accompany this game bird. Ideal ways of serving are: 1. In a nest of Chestnut Purée. 2. On Buttered Toast. 3. On toast spread with Purée of Cooked Calf's Liver moistened with Sherry.

Squab, Roasted or Broiled: Serve with Currant Jelly and—if offered as a main course at a luncheon—with light vegetables, Mushrooms, Peas, Beans, Asparagus on Toast, Spinach in Puff Paste or Fried Potato Balls.

Boiled Ham: For Boiled Ham Champagne or Cider Sauce is best. Potatoes in practically any form desired, Creamed, Chantilly, Escalloped, *etc.*, with Spinach, Beet Greens, Cauliflower, Brussels Sprouts are vegetable choices.

Pork: Implies the presence of the apple, as Apple Sauce, Cider Apple Sauce, Fried Apples or Apple Croquettes, though Sauce Soubise or Sauce Piquant may also be used with it. Potatoes, if desired, and practically any vegetable are in order.

Roast Veal: A Brown Gravy or Sauce Soubise are proper for veal. Rice, Spaghetti, Macaroni, are accompanying dishes; and practically all the usual garden vegetables are in order.

Roast Venison: A Wild Plum Sauce is especially appropriate, plus Currant Jelly. Potatoes should be Saratoga or French Fried. French String Beans and French Peas, Brussels Sprouts (with Chestnuts) and Mushrooms (in Brown Madeira Sauce) will add to the occasion.

CHAPTER XII
MENUS FOR A THANKSGIVING—A CHRISTMAS AND A LENTEN DINNER

[From "A Book of Good Dinners for My Friend." FANNY MERRITT FARMER.]

THANKSGIVING DINNER

Clam Soup, Browned Crackers. Halibut Rolls, Sauce Tartare, Dressed Cucumbers. Roast Turkey with Chestnut Stuffing, Giblet Gravy, Maître d'Hotel Potatoes. Mashed Winter Squash, Onions in Cream, Cranberry Punch. Pear Salad, French Dressing, Thanksgiving Pudding, Hard Sauce, Vanilla Ice Cream, Hot Chocolate Sauce, Sponge Cake, Assorted Nuts, Fruit, Black Coffee.

CHRISTMAS DINNER

Clam and Tomato Consommé. Browned Soup Rings. Olives and Salted Pecans. Fillets of Sole, Mushroom Sauce. Roast Goose, Giblet Gravy, Frozen Apples. Riced Potatoes, Glazed Silver Skins. Pimento Timbales. Chiffonade Salad. English Plum Pudding, Sherry Sauce. Coffee Ice Cream, Almond Cakes. Bonbons. Crackers and Cheese. Black Coffee.

LENTEN DINNER

Smoked Salmon and Anchovy Canapés. Tomato Bisque Soup. Buttered Croquettes, Croutons. Tartlets of Egg with Curry. Boiled Cod, Venetian Sauce. Hot Potato Salad. Cauliflower au Gratin. Cheese Soufflé. Chocolate Bavarian Cream. Black Coffee.

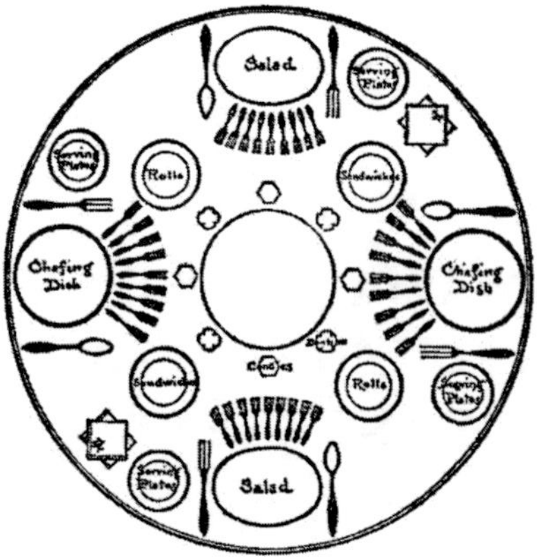

[DIAGRAM OF A BUFFET TABLE]

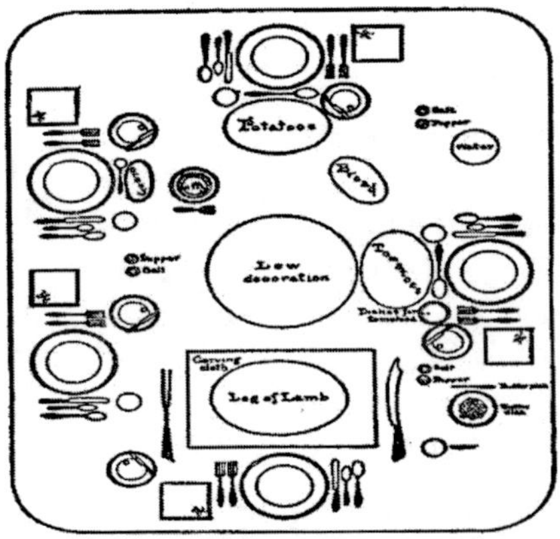

[DIAGRAM OF TABLE LAID FOR HOME DINNER WITHOUT SERVICE OF MAID]

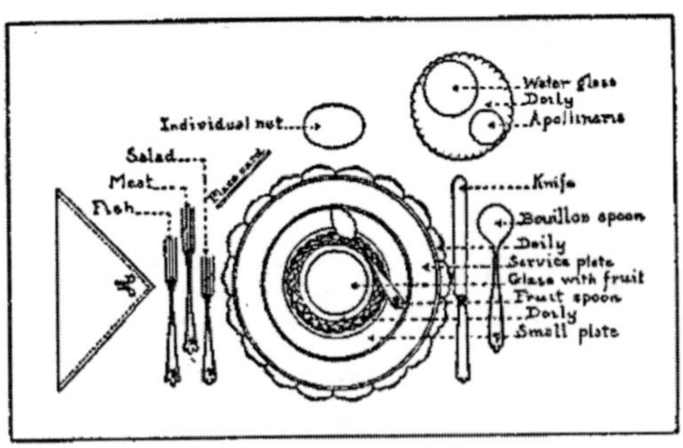

[LUNCHEON COVER IN DETAIL]

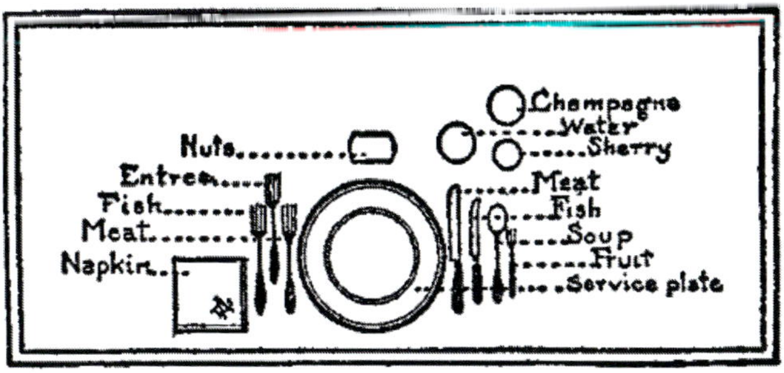

[FORMAL DINNER COVER IN DETAIL]

INTERIOR DECORATION

CHAPTER I
LINES AND CURVES

Straight lines in a room call for straight lines in furniture, rugs and hangings. They make a room dignified and serious in appearance. Italian Renaissance chairs and other pieces of that period, and our modern Craftsman and Mission chairs (often hard and stiff examples of the straight-line type of furniture, just as Bokhara, Kazan and Afghan rugs are of the straight-line rug) are furniture of this kind. The severe line is also produced by velvet draperies topped by straight-lined lambrequins. A straight line is to be preferred to a weak curve. And it is usually possible to redeem too straight and rigid an appearance in furniture by relieving long, straight lines (as in tables) by carved ornamentation and the application of curved lines on a secondary plane, i. e., in parts of the legs. In general, when not too rigid, straight lines in interior decoration stand for repose, sobriety and dignity.

CURVED LINES

Curved lines in decoration and furniture are of various kinds. The rococo styles (Louis XV and the Regency) are overluxurious and often weak; the curves in Arabic or Celtic ornamentation vague and obscure. The undulating curves of Persian rugs suggest movement. Curves, in general, which turn *up*, make an effect of animation and happiness. Wall papers and draperies used to emphasize such furniture curves lend an air of happy animation to the rooms in which they are used.

Contrast to stiff, straight lines is afforded by the use of the curved line in decoration, which offers soft, rich and lovely effects. In general, curved lines make for grace, flexibility and softness.

BROKEN LINES

Broken lines give us a feeling of life and movement. But they should not be used for the permanent decorative lines of a room—the lines of the walls, openings, hangings, draperies, carpets, or large, immovable pieces of furniture which have a fixed place. In pillows which break the long back line of a couch, in cornice moldings, lambrequin bottoms, chair backs, screens, *etc.*, they lend life. But as a rule they should be sparingly used.

VERTICAL LINES

Vertical lines express aspiration and disquietude; diagonal lines, action. In wall paper designs and rug patterns the diagonal line is not always excellent. Diagonal lines are sometimes effective in rugs; but the feeling of energetic movement they produce in wall papers or drop patterns is objectionable. It annoys the eye and is usually inartistic.

CHAPTER II
FORM, COLOR AND PROPORTION

Never overemphasize one of the dimensions of *height, width* and *depth* at the expense of one of the others. They must be harmonized.

OBLONG

The proportions of any room are best when they make a normal impression on the eye. The oblong is the best decorative art *form,* as a rule. It can be used in nearly all ornaments, in walls, doors and windows, ceilings and floors, in rugs and furniture, because it is obvious.

THE SQUARE

The square form is solid and firm, but tends to be monotonous. Square windows, fireplaces and wall spaces, as well as square rooms in general and pictures, are usually uninteresting, and this applies to cubes as well. The big cubical chair, for instance, is something to be avoided.

THE TRIANGLE

The triangular form (in mantel clocks, lampshades, highboys, bookcase foundations, and sometimes where it appears in wall paper or Turcoman rug designs) expresses movement in repose admirably, and has real decorative values.

CURVED FORMS

Curved forms, the circle, the oval and the ellipse, are all agreeable. There is in them "a hint of the mysterious dualism of life."

COLOR

Colors makes decorative shapes easy to see. (For the character of the colors and the principles of their effective combination the reader will find much useful information in the "Color Harmony and Design in Dress" included in this series.) Art, Nature and books will all help the interior decorator in the matter of color adjustment. Trim in most houses compels the adjustment of the color harmony to suit it. In general white paneling calls for the use of one warm and one cool color, while dark brown or black paneling needs two or more warm colors.

PROPORTION

All parts of a furnished room must help express one ideal of balance. The realization of this ideal is proportion. A horizontal room calls for horizontal furniture and lines, a vertical room for vertical ones. Every important decorative feature of a room must be selected in accordance with its proportion in general. The size of a room increases the form scale (or scale of the forms) represented by furniture, pictures, rugs, *etc*. In every room the important individual pieces, such as library table, piano, bed, dresser, must parallel one or another wall. Do not violate proportion and artistic effect by overcrowding.

CHAPTER III
INDIVIDUAL ROOMS OF THE HOUSE

THE DINING ROOM AND "WORK ROOMS"

The dining room, with which we were so directly concerned in the preceding portion of this book, offers a natural point of departure for considering the individual rooms of the house with regard to decoration. First, as to a dominant dining room color: The dining room should be a room of good cheer, a bright, happy room. But it should not be too bright. If it is on the sunny side of the house, let one of the colors dominate—white, cream white, blues, greens, grays or violet— if on the shady side, gain warmth by the use of yellows (save lemon), orange, warm tans, russets, pinks, yellowish greens and reds. (This applies to all rooms.)

Do not use restless-patterned wall papers. Leather (used with paneling or above wainscot), modern tapestries, fabrics of all kinds are suitable for covering dining-room walls. If low, the ceiling should never be dark, since this makes the room appear still lower. (A breakfast room done in lacquer is very effective, however, if not too low.) A single large rug, harmonizing with the wall color scheme is admirable in any room. In the dining room, however, a figured carpet is often preferred for practical reasons: it stands wear and tear around the table better. Well-chosen paper (See Chapter II) often improves a badly proportioned room by optical illusion. The ideal lightings for dining rooms are side lights. Dining-room drop lights or domes are very trying to the eyes of those who dine, and are unbecoming. Side lights (adding candles for grace and charm) are far pleasanter to the eyes and look better.

In the dining room the table is the dominating furniture note. A round table, an oblong table or a square table may be the more desirable according to the shape of the room. But a round dining table may be harmonized with an oblong dining room by means of an oblong rug, with rounded medallion, by a round flower bowl, a round tray or even the wheels of the tea table. In the dining room, as elsewhere, repetition in color establishes the color tone of the room. In the dining room, as elsewhere, every individual room presents an individual case, to be worked out decoratively in accordance with the principles already given. One more color hint regarding the dining room, drawn from a modern authority: "When we think of the ideal dinner—the soft lights, the hospitable warmth, the sparkle of crystal, the gleam of silver, the quick talk and gay laughter of the guests—we think of *red,* for that color is indissolubly bound in thought with the idea of richness, hospitality and excitement." Yet red, as we will see later, is a color to be used with great caution.

WORKING ROOMS VERSUS LIVING ROOMS

Before passing to the other rooms of the house, we will pause to consider a more purely utilitarian group.

The Kitchen.—These rooms which are strictly utilitarian, more or less escape decorative control. The kitchen, aside from the elements of proportion in arrangement of its furnishings, is not properly a room for decoration. A cheerful color, plenty of light—a practical essential—and practical arrangement of its furniture and equipment are of more importance than the decorative element. Neatness, color harmony and a restful eye effect should be obtained. This applies as well to the butler's pantry. Pantry and kitchen should always be shut off from the dining room, so that the latter's decorative values are not affected by them.

The Bathroom.—Tiled or hardwood flooring, painted or glazed washable walls, sanitary plumbing, glass shelves, washable cotton rugs and bath mats, all the modern conveniences in keeping with the purposes of the room, thrust the decorative element into the background. The curtains must be simple and quite easily washed.

The Home Sewing Room.—The home sewing room, too, may be viewed decoratively as well as practically. A sunny room with western exposure, kalsomined in pale warm gray, the floor covered with cream-colored matting, windows fitted with white Holland shades—a combination restful to the eye—and furnished with hard-wood framed, cane-bottomed chairs.

CHAPTER IV
LIVING ROOM, DRAWING ROOM AND LIBRARY

We now return to the rooms where decoration is the rule. While always remembering that connecting rooms must harmonize with one another in color, individual colors may always be appropriately chosen for certain rooms, because they express the dominant mood and character of the room in question. Thus, for the living room or drawing room, the yellows, oranges and golden browns, which combine the cheer of yellow and the warmth of red, are excellent. If a restful instead of a cheerful quality is desired for the living room or drawing room, green may be made the dominant hue. Yellow is a joyous tint, also a good breakfast-room hue. It will harmonize in the living room with plain fumed oak, willow furniture and cretonne hangings as well as with painted and paneled ivory walls, old Chinese rugs, damask hangings and satinwood and lacquered furniture. But furniture, bric-a-brac and walls always *must* be good in line and color. For proper floor balance use a large rug in a large living room, and several small ones in a small one. Furniture, too, should be chosen in view of the emphasis each individual piece has; and its relations to the room in general. The effect of stiffness is not overcome by placing heavy pieces of furniture askew in a room. Yet this is often done. Scale and proportion should always dictate the choice of furniture, lamps and pictures. Each has its place in the general decorative scheme. Red is a hard color for the eyes. Many a red living room has been the cause of chronic headache. Not that red need be entirely tabooed. A living room for example, paneled in oak, with a soft red-toned Oriental rug, red draperies, a touch of red in a stained glass window panel, and red cushioned window seat will have far more warmth and charm than a room whose walls are completely covered with red.

The Hall and Library.—Red, however, makes a hall seem hospitable and full of welcome. It is also a good library color. In halls where walls are papered or paneled with stripes or draperies rich red may appear in the ground of an Oriental rug on the floor, and be matched in the hue of the portières or stair runner. With damask or tapestry, or large-figured duplex papered hall walls, a soft-toned red rug, with hangings and stair runner matching it, is best. The walls should show a neutral tint, and red will dominate with pleasing effect.

In the library, in winter, with a glow from the open fire playing over a red rug, "revealing shadowy outline of bookcases, and dim velvet draperies, as a deep-shaded lamp throws a beam of light over the arm of a big reading chair," red seems indeed an ideal color for the room.

CHAPTER V
BED ROOM, NURSERY AND PLAY ROOM

For the bedroom, though other colors such as green and violet, in particular (save red, which is a poor bedroom hue) are not barred, blue is an ideal color, expressive of repose and tranquil ease. In the bedroom, however, as in all other rooms, the light and location must always be considered in establishing the color note. Curtains either make or mar a room, especially a bedroom. Bedroom curtains, whether of expensive or cheap material, must emphasize the restful charm of the room. If a bedroom (or other room) is plain in color, the curtains may be either plain or figured. But it is dangerous when wall designs of bedrooms is apt to convey a feeling of restlessness. The bedroom may be provided with one large or several smaller rugs as a floor covering, according to size. Plain rugs are more restful in effect, and with plain walls and chintz often present a charming effect.

NURSERY AND PLAY ROOM

These children's rooms should always give out a gay and cheerful atmosphere. To obtain this wall papers with colorful friezes with characters from fairy tale, Mother Goose or Noah's Ark, may be used above a simple wainscot. Painted walls with stenciled designs are also attractive. Small chairs and tables with good lines, a bookcase, a toy cupboard, a sand table, and window boxes where the children may plant seeds, are all possible decorative units of such a room. The general color scheme must be soft and cheerful, plain linoleum is the best floor covering, the few pictures should hang low, and the window curtains should be of white muslin, with side hangings (down to sill) with some special nursery design in cretonne.

CHAPTER VI
SOME HINTS ANENT PERIOD FURNITURE

Period furniture is a means to a decorative end. It is a *part* of the decoration of a room, and must be adapted to its lines and proportions. Halls for instance, call for tall chairs and cabinets and long and narrow wall tables. Pictures and bric-a-brac are out of place in the hall. In the living room, where spaciousness and repose are wanted, substantial, comfortable chairs, long, low sofas, cabinets and tables, and no fussy furniture adjuncts are demanded. Similarly in the dining room, the furniture lines should make the room a more comfortable and restful one in which to eat; and bedroom furniture must in all decorative ways carry out the idea of rest and sleeping. If period furniture is used, the drawing room usually gives the dominant note, which should be carried out (in more or less modified form) throughout the other rooms. Do not make too abrupt contrasts in using period furniture. Late Louis XVI and Early Empire have much in common. But it is a shock to find Louis XV and Late Empire in the same room. Sheraton and Rococo, Early Jacobean oak and late eighteenth century English mahogany do not mix. If your rooms are Colonial use Colonial or Georgian styles of furniture. For ball rooms, small reception rooms, and the boudoirs of blooming young beauty—not those of dignified old age—Louis XV is to be commended. Formal dining rooms stand Louis XV and Louis XVI styles very well. On the other hand the simple beauty of line of Adam, Sheraton, Heppelwhite and Chippendale are better suited to simpler rooms—though they may be quite as subtly and perfectly finished. In general, the choice of all furniture—chairs, tables, beds, mirrors—should be influenced by the size of the house and rooms, individual circumstances and individual taste, where the last does not conflict with established laws of decoration.

CONCLUSION

Interior Decoration is a very extensive and complicated subject. What we have here attempted to do has been to give an idea of the general principles underlying it, together with as many direct and practical hints and suggestions as has been possible within the limits allotted. It is hoped that they may lead the reader to take a more personal interest in a fascinating subject of study. If this be the case, a large number of specialized works which treat every least phase of "Interior Decoration" in exhaustive detail, are available.